The Colors of
My Sister

Kailyn McMahon-Boggess
Wallflower Writing

BookLeaf Publishing
India | USA | UK

Presentation by *BookLeaf Publishing*

Web: www.bookleafpub.com

E-mail: info@bookleafpub.com

ISBN: 9789360944735

First edition 2024

For Casey Jones, my chosen sister.

*For anyone who has experienced grief, and
who will continue to. You are not alone.*

ACKNOWLEDGEMENT

Wallflower Writing was created as a way to express emotions and communication through written rhetoric.

I would like to acknowledge Justina Carver, my caring friend through life, who continues to wade with me in the depths of impossible grief. She pushes me to continue to write and create, at times when I have felt it would be impossible to express myself, bearing the weight of grief. I would not have been brave enough to bear the weight of my soul out loud, without the support of my friend.

I would like to acknowledge my husband, Scott who encourages me with loving kindness and lets me drop my armor, allowing me to flourish. To my sweet and charming daughter, Autumn, who inspires me to seek joy and whom Casey Jones would be so, so proud of.

PREFACE

Of all the friends I ever had, *she* was the most colorful. You couldn't put just one color on her.

Though she might have told you once or twice it was cerulean blue, she was a full-spectrum rainbow.

Then one day - it all felt sad-blue.

Like a sea of thousand forget-me-nots, each one, a regret, a should-have-been, an 'as a matter of fact you did this poorly' reminder.

Blue - the hue of tears, an empty sky and blue, the hue of sadness.

Blue, like my sister's favorite color.

She

She is the person who knows all about the ways my heart has been broken.

She is the one who knows all the ways it is surely bound to break again.

She is the unbreakable bond you feel when you trust me, the cumulative lessons that have made me who I am.

She is the person who wrote history with me and still opens that book, revisits it, and takes new insight.

She is the steadfast investment you feel when you're loved by me, a familiar embrace that has shifted and shaped my depth of love.

She is the person I clung to when I searched for my identity as an individual, the one who wasn't sour when I claimed it.

She is the person who wades with me in the pits of grief, who grabs my hand tightly in the shallows and makes me promise to hold on.

She is who comes when you open your heart to
the way you deserve to be loved.

When you are convinced by me that there is still
good in this world - it is because I was
convinced by her.

My Chosen Sister

The first time I saw her, I felt whole.

Like the empty caverns and caves of my soul
were filled up by her laughter.

And every moment that I had her, I was whole.

She was a blend of everyone she ever loved, and
would often compliment our most impressive
qualities.

Her love was messy, big and bold and it filled up
my holes.

She was a rainbow in a way that she would
blend herself into you, and share your goodness
like a tapestry in the sky.

She made you feel larger than life.

She took up space to laugh, to tell stories, and
she would sing.

She knew that her purpose was to share her gifts and her colors with the world. So, she shared them freely.

Like a rainbow spans the sky for all to see, she naturally demanded the attention of the room.

She filled silent spaces with thoughtful musings.

She talked so much and not enough.

There are almost no words, and not enough words at the same time, to accurately describe the essence of *her.*

She would ease through fashion trends and cigarettes, and you never knew which colorful mood you were going to get.

Every alter ego and phase she adhered to, matched a stronger sense of autonomy, authenticity and freewill.

She was colorful, in a world that really needed that.

Every color was magnificent, and every color infected each person she would meet.

Eventually casting her a net of just as colorful personalities to love her back.

A rainbow of people who would all love her, for her.

She was the storm and the sunshine.

She was the water and the light.

She was mine.

My chosen sister - gone too soon from a world that really needed her.

Hurricane

If we could see our cosmic story before we're gone, do you think we would even notice all the quirky calculated fates that occur as they are occurring?

I read a bit about a married couple who discovered they were in each other's photos on the same day and time without even knowing each other.

Back then, dozens of years before marrying, they were simply wandering strangers. But all those years later, they would learn of this moment where they were together, before they were ever really together. *A simple twist of fate.*

Is that what "destiny" is? Or, were they just lucky enough to find out before it was "too late"?

We don't all take out the camera and get the shot to make time stand still; there is not always proof of the events and steps that led to an outcome.

Maybe not even after you're gone.

But if you could have a cosmic overview of your story, would you even really want it anyway?

I don't think I would.

Because that would mean we saw the end before it happened, and nobody saw this ending coming.

But to best understand the ending, it is very important that you fully grasp this beginning.

It started with a rainbow that we all knew and loved.

Then one day, it turned into a *hurricane*.

You don't always know the steps it takes to lead to the outcome.

All we can do is look for the signs.

Red

Red - like a flame.

A flicker of fascination -
A flashy and magnetic pull.

The allure to be different -
To be the first to taste it.

A fleeting moment.
A good time to have and a story to tell.

Red, the forbidden fruit,
And the curiosity to taste it.

Red, the color of my sister.

Orange

Orange - a hue of hesitation.

Handcrafted excuses.
A hue of denial.

One more taste -
One more try.

A tangled web.
Hushed goodbyes.

Masked,
Behind a façade of control.

Orange, a hue that ignites.
Orange, the color of my sister.

Yellow

Yellow, an inviting light.
Caution light, awareness dawns.

The warning signs flicker, like a blinking yellow.
Fleeting moments of clarity.

A hesitant recognition.

So close, you can taste it.
So, you taste it.

A yellow brick road, calling you to play.

Yellow, the color of my sister.

Green

Green - a vibrant depth.
A semblance of control wavers.

Vulnerability persists.
Attempts to moderate mend a breaking soul.

A wish for resolve.
A plea for salvation.

Green, a light for proceeding.

Green, the color of my sister.

Blue

12

Blue - a deep, deep sea.
With this hue, descent deepens.

An ache to dismiss and nowhere to share.
You head for the cave, and no one comes in.

A sorrowful sigh -
A yearning unseen.

Blue, like a sea of thousand forget-me-nots.

Blue, like my sister's favorite color.

Indigo

13

Indigo - like a tranquil dusk.
The grip gets loose.

The last glimmer of possibility.
Indigo, like ink - vast on a canvas.

A stirring desire for change,
In the depths of deep despair.

Indigo, the color of the fight.

Indigo, the color of my sister.

Violet

Violet - the end or the beginning.
A secret plea. A silent fight.

Surrendering to the truth how it takes you.
However it takes you.

Confronting the demons,
While they confront you.

Violet, the end of the rainbow.

And violet, the final color of my sister.

She's Gone

"She's gone."

"She's gone."

"She's gone."

I read it over and over again.

Trying to understand what it could mean. I
thought out loud, "She's wasted and
drunk-kind-of gone."

I told myself different stories.
I painted a picture in my head of her, having run
off to the store.

Disbelief denied what inside I already knew was
the truth: "She is really gone."

It rang through my ears drums,
It perused through my veins.

"She's gone."

"She's gone."

"She's gone."

The time flashed. I once thought it was long,
being half my life involved - it turned into
minutes.

As if the lifetime we made together was flying
by on a reel in millisecond-screenshots, my heart
knowing that's all that it ever would be again-
broke.

All of me did, into a million little pieces that
would never be repaired.

There are hollows in your chest, when you feel
like your heart is actually breaking.

It's beating and it's there, but somehow at the
same time, it's just a hollow space that used to
beat.
Where she used to beat with me, before she was
gone.

A hollow space of sound.

"She's gone."

"She's gone."

"She's gone."

I knew then, she was never coming back.

Only Knowing

We would sit there, waiting.
Sorting photos, occasionally falling to the floor.

We'd pace around the cold rental house for what
felt like both a year and a blink. Waiting.

The floors would creek and the wind would
blow hard against the antique glass window
panes.

Some days the sun would shine.
But most of those days, it did not.

At night we would sit at the table before bed.
A lot of the time in silence, a candle burning and
a cup of tea. *She* loved tea.

We would sit and we would wait. Once and a
while the dogs would make us resistantly smile.

Or someone brave enough would not heed
demands of isolation and they'd come in with
food and hugs, and they would stay too long.
And we wait for them to leave.

At night when the tea was done and the lights
were going down, the dogs would find their beds
and each of us would find ours.

We would lay our heads and we would wait.

The room between us - and the space between -
would make the time we spend soaking it all in
together feel too far away.

Without *her*, everything felt too far away.

In the night, the howls would come roaring
through the creaky wind-beaten walls, sounding
off the belly cries of grief-struck friendship.

The moon would shine through the spare room
window on my face, and each reminder of my
given life would leave me howling more for the
loss of hers.

Each echo met by my other half - whom all
those years before had been one-third before this
loss- in the room across from me.

Each, a reminder of all nights of the rest of our
lives that were yet to come, without our dearest
friend.

It felt as if we were 'in waiting'.
Maybe death is just a game.
I repeat, this is not a sham.

But the sun would rise and we would too.

No longer waiting. *Only knowing.*

Ambiguous Reality

When it rains, *that's a sign*. It's true what they
say, to look for the signs. Whether a sign to roll
your windows up, or put on a raincoat, some
would call that a *sign*.

But they never clearly say just what you're
supposed to do when you see the signs.

Or, how they might look different on someone
you just never really *could* paint one color.

They say now, that if you aren't anti-racist,
you're a part of the problem. I agree.

And so, I have to wonder if you aren't actively
following your friends into the cave - maybe
you're a part of the problem, too.

Somedays, the regrets run immense.
Others, the confusion consoles the regret.

A million different people will tell us, "You
can't hold that weight." To them, I would
respond, "All the other times, *we did*."

Albert Hofman says that:
"What one commonly takes as 'the reality' ... by no means signifies something fixed, but rather, something that is ambiguous…
There are many realities."

The sun would rise another day, but my dearest friend did not. That was this new and painful reality.

Even without knowing, we always somehow know.

And maybe that is why we feel so *very* deeply.

Maybe all along - we are supposed to find our people and *feel* our people.

We are to field through all the rotten ones and do the hard work, until you understand the *why*.

We are to find the good ones, and then help them field through their rotten situations.

Maybe, it's just hard to see the signs when you see so much love.

There is no fixed reality, only ambiguous ones.

Never Coming Back

Another 365 days around the sun and she's not here. She is still gone.

The winter cold is coming and it comes quickly and colder every year that she is gone.

At first, I would be tricked by my thoughts: "She is coming back. This is just a sham." But the days come and keep coming, and she does not. This is not a sham. She is really gone.

To some, she is just a story I tell and that I will continue telling.

To some, she is just a thought and a photograph by now.

To some, she is just a memory.

But to me, she beats in my chest.

Another week, another year, another decade will pass, and I will still blink my eyelids with each necessary blink.

She etched into the backs of them, replaying, remaking, reliving, and holding tightly to each moment I ever had before it was gone.

Before she was never coming back.

Another Half

She was the friend I had for over half my life.

When we were growing up I never imagined a lifetime that didn't have her in it.

And then one day just like that, one day out of the blue, this lifetime would never have her in it again.

Some people say that absence makes the heart grow fonder and I don't know if that's true or not.

But, what I do know is that I am still just as destroyed as I was the night I realized that life would go on without her.

The constant want to tell her something or share a memory with her didn't just go away. It comes as frequently as it ever did, but now instead of turning to *her* to share it, I just try not to cry.

The tendency to include her never stopped, and talking about her in past tense never has gotten easier.

I still talk to her most days.
But she doesn't talk back to me.

I miss the way she knew me and the way only
she knew to love me.

I miss the belly laughs.

A vault of my secrets left when she did.
And a part of my history too.

I was as changed by her departure as I was
bonded to her arrival.
We were one.

I still feel called to love her even when I can't
always feel her calling back.

Constant reminders of her bring joy and
subsequential pain.

Every reminder meets me hastily at the threshold
of loving her and losing her, *over and over
again.*

We used to say so proudly that we knew each
other for over half of our lives.

But as mine continues to go on, I live with
pervasive thoughts of knowing it was only ever
half for her.

I will spend the rest of mine wondering who she
would have been if she at least had another half.

I Accept It

Grief is a lifelong journey.

Here we are now, trying to paint light in a dark world - that for us - used to always be a rainbow.

Today still, we are picking up the pieces of an irreparable loss.
We always will be.

All these years later, still trying to navigate this unforgiving world with undone stitches in the fabric of our messy, undone souls.

Grief is a heavy burden to bear.

Here we are at the end, walking through the rainbow.

Finally grasping that it is purely a reflection and refraction of the life and color that lay just on the other side.

I accept that once we walk through, from the other side, *all the color dies.*

I know that to move forward after the rain, I
must accept a sunny day.

This loss is a part of who I am as much as her
life is a part of who I am.

Grief is as unending as love.
One day, we must *accept* it.

I accept it.

I Will Wonder

I will always wonder…

Could I have loved you better?
Could I have tried harder?

I will wonder...

Could I have said it differently?
Done things....differently?

But you can not.
I know that I can not.

It's not up to us who stays or who goes.
It's not up to you to change the past.

It's scary to be vulnerable -
Even scarier to live in regret.

The thing is, none of us get to stay forever.
Not one of us. No one gets out alive.

It's up to you to love your people and your life.
And even though I know that -

I will always wonder why I can not have her
back.

I will always wonder who she would have been.

I will always wonder how I can love the next
humans in my life the way I loved her and more.

I will always wonder *why*.

But I know that some things are not meant for us
to hold.

Lean

Lean into who you love.

Hold tight to what you know.
When the world is forced to go to sleep -
look around and lean into your own.

Lean.

Let them fill your voids and spaces.
Let them calm your fears.
You can't do it all alone.
Let them feel you *here*.

Lean into them.

In a world constantly searching for answers -
Excelling through the unknown - *lean*
Grief is unending,
Lean into those you love.

You can not do this all alone.

Lean.

Greater Love

It's hard to think about the cosmic view of the world, and a rainbow or your life, when this can all so quickly be taken from you.

Growing up, we didn't know how good we had it. I don't think any child does.

Our best friends were a short run away.

The bus stop was a place to meet your lifelong friend and you would meet there for half of your life.

Or at least if you're lucky, like me, you can get almost half your life.

They say to go through grief, you must go through each of the seasons, and great loss makes you think about every interaction you've ever had.

Each challenge, every triumph, every single season.

At first, you watch the people around you, just
as desperate and confused.

Then you will laugh at the stories, and make no
doubt, you will cry again.

Knowing it's the last time you'll ever be with
someone you love, you'll whimper, scream or
even fall to your knees.

And you will again, and again.

Yet, as time goes, you will discover that even in
the changing of seasons, and with new
perspectives coming each day, the immeasurable
void remains entirely the same.

From the funeral to the grave,
the 1st-anniversary date to the 20th, the depth of
the pain remains unchanged.

So with each fall and with each season, you will
rise and you will walk again.
Until the next season that brings you to your
knees. And it will again, and again.

Great grief does not tire through just one year of
seasons - *it takes you* - for all of the rest of them.
It's great love with no exit sign, all this grieving.

So, when they say, "It takes a year or seasons",
please understand that saying "goodbye" to
someone you love for the last time, is also
saying "hello" to your new self for the first time.

Because it is not just the final season of their
life, but also the *first* season of the rest of yours.

The truth is, there is no agenda for loss.
No timeframe for recovery, and no amount of
seasons that will make it different.

There is only trusting in your heart that to have
been afforded great grief, we were *lucky* to have
first been afforded even greater love.

After the Rain

There isn't anything I haven't learned from this loss. And every minute, I learn more.

I've learned everything from how to operate without one of my legs to keep myself here when I really thought I wanted to die.

I've learned how to show up in the world when I am showing up in the *shell* of a hurt person. And how to keep my head up, when it was too heavy to even hold.

She was such a huge part of me, that even now I wonder how anyone could think that I was the same as I've ever been, knowing that she is gone.

It hurts to think the ones who know me now, will never fully understand who I was when she was *here*.

If we are truly the sum of all of the people that we meet and of all of our experiences, then I haven't been 'myself' since she's been gone.

I used to cry about the days and how long they
were.

I didn't think the right amount of minutes and
seconds added up to how much time had passed
since I lost her.

2,555 days without my chosen sister - my first
ever best friend.
Not a single one of them got by me.
Not a single second ever will.

It takes knowing grief to understand it.
I wouldn't wish it on my worst enemy.

It's an everlasting gut punch even when you're
smiling.

Grief does not slow down or let up.
No matter how quiet those around you are about
it, it's always a thing they're going through.

Even if you think enough time has passed, it
hasn't. *It never will.*

You could be looking me dead in the eyes and I
could tell you I am fine, but inside, I am missing
my friend and I always will be.

They say time heals all things, but I'm still waiting.

I'm not the same - I never will be.

After the rain, you pray for a rainbow.

But you never forget the hurricane, and you never forget the rain.

Over The Rainbow - Epilogue

We can see the cosmic story before we go - if we choose to. If we look for the signs and search for the colors.

Everything can be calculated with love, and the things that you need to make a rainbow are served freely to each of us in this world if only we reach out and find it.

We must have the courage to accept what is meant for us, even when we don't want it. Just the same way that we accept the weather and a rainbow.

She is gone.

But she will never really *be* gone.

She knew as only her colorful soul could insistently know- that teardrops and light at the end of the tunnel - would make rainbows for the world.

So, she went on, making rainbows for the world.